mirrors of time

Also by Brian L. Weiss, M.D.

Many Lives, Many Masters

Meditation: *Achieving Inner Peace and Tranquility in Your Life* (available May 2002)

Messages from the Masters: *Tapping into the Power of Love*

Only Love Is Real: *A Story of Soulmates Reunited*

Through Time into Healing

Healing the Mind and Spirit Cards
(available February 2003)

mirrors
of time

Using Regression for Physical,
Emotional, and Spiritual Healing

Brian L. Weiss, M.D.

Hay House, Inc.
Carlsbad, California • Sydney, Australia
Canada • Hong Kong • United Kingdom

Copyright © 2002 by Brian Weiss

Published and distributed in the United States by:
Hay House, Inc., P.O. Box 5100, Carlsbad, CA 92018-5100
(800) 654-5126 • (800) 650-5115 (fax) • www.hayhouse.com
Hay House Australia Pty Ltd, P.O. Box 515, Brighton-Le-Sands NSW
2216 • *phone:* 1800 023 516 • *e-mail:* info@hayhouse.com.au

Editorial supervision: Jill Kramer • *Design:* Summer McStravick

Cataloging-in-Publication Data
available from the Library of Congress

ISBN 1-56170-929-8

05 04 03 02   4 3 2 1
1st printing, February 2002

Printed in the United States of America

Contents

Introduction

Over the past 20 years, I've used meditation and regression techniques with thousands of patients, helping many of them alleviate psychological *and* physical symptoms. The benefits of meditation, healing visualization, and regression have been extensively documented in my previous books; in addition, my CDs have helped many people achieve states of inner peace and tranquility.

Mirrors of Time allows you to take the next step. Using the CD included within, you can now actually undergo the same regression techniques that I use with my patients. Now *you* can go back through time to remember past events that may have led to the symptoms or difficulties you're experiencing today. Through the process of remembering these past events, current symptoms will tend to diminish, and a strong sense of peace and well-being will likely emerge. Sometimes the memories evoked will be of childhood or in utero incidents—but, if you feel that you need to experience past-life memories in order to resolve current life problems, they, too, can be elicited by the exercises on the CD.

The benefits of regression therapy extend far beyond the alleviation of symptoms. Healing often results on all levels of our being, including the physical, the emotional, and the spiritual. Just about every one of my patients practices meditation and/or regression exercises between their visits to my office—for the more they practice, the faster and deeper they can go. The exercises on the CD are very safe, and thousands of people have been using them over the years. However, it's extremely important that you be patient even if you don't notice immediate results. Regular practice will foster your physical and emotional health and will open up spiritual vistas that can endow your life with new meaning.

I hope that through the practice of these exercises, you will feel more joy, peace, and love in your life.

PART I

egression

Chapter One

Healing the Body,

Touching the Soul

*I*n 1992, in order to further document the importance and efficacy of regression therapy, I wrote *Through Time into Healing*. At that time, I had already helped hundreds of patients retrieve childhood and past-life memories, a process that often led to very rapid and dramatic clinical improvement. Since then, the number of patients I've treated has reached more than 3,000, and I have conducted workshops and seminars in many countries. Many of the participants at these events have also had their present disorders improve as they recalled their past-life experiences.

I have written another book called *Meditation: Achieving Inner Peace and Tranquility in Your Life* (to be published by Hay House in May 2002), which is about using meditation for deep relaxation and healing. In *Mirrors of Time,* however, I want to specifically concentrate on regression exercises.

The efficacy of regression therapy in curing symptoms—such as fears and phobias that originated in earlier incarnations—has been extensively validated over the years. But I personally found, as my work expanded, that I was able to discover other benefits of this type of therapy, whether people were in my office or using the CDs I created. I initially recorded these exercises to offer my patients a way of continuing to

4

develop their powers of concentration at home so that they could access their subconscious memories between therapy sessions. I noted that the more my patients practiced, the faster they were able to reach deep states of relaxation and concentration in the one-on-one sessions we had in my office.

However, I also became aware that regression exercises practiced regularly can unlock energies within people that they're usually unaware of. I want to emphasize these additional benefits and encourage you to acquire a practice that will foster your physical and emotional health, which will open up spiritual vistas that can endow your life with new and profound meaning.

Many questions have been addressed to me regarding the practice of regression therapy. The following chapters should alleviate any concerns you may have about reincarnation, regression therapy, hypnosis, or the risks of doing the regression exercises by yourself. In this way, you can reap the full

benefit of the exercises; for when the blocks and obstacles are removed, not only will physical and emotional symptoms improve, but barriers to your inner
peace and happiness will also disappear.

Chapter Two

My Own Beginnings

*I*f this is the first time you're reading one of my books, it's important that you know a little about my professional background, and how my skepticism has gradually evolved into a more open-minded attitude. (I describe this extensively in my first book, *Many Lives, Many Masters,* but I'll give you a brief overview here.)

I graduated from Columbia University and received my medical degree from Yale University School of Medicine, where I also completed my residency training in psychiatry. I taught at several highly respected medical schools, and I also published more than 40 scientific papers, mainly in the field of psychopharmacology and sleep disorders. When the experience took place that changed my entire outlook on life, I was chairman of the Department of Psychiatry at Mount Sinai Medical Center, a teaching hospital affiliated with the University of Miami. I was an academic psychiatrist, utterly skeptical about what I considered "nonscientific areas." I knew nothing about the concept of reincarnation, and didn't have the slightest interest in the subject.

Then I started to treat Catherine, a woman in her late 20s who was suffering from depression, phobias, and panic attacks. A year of conventional psychotherapy had produced no results, which prompted me to try hypnosis—I felt that recalling her repressed childhood traumas might explain her current symptoms. But despite uncovering several traumatic incidents from her childhood, she still failed to improve. I continued using hypnosis, looking for even earlier childhood traumas. I instructed her to go back to the time and the events that caused her phobias. To my complete amazement, she went back approximately *4,000 years* to a former life in the Middle East. Catherine then started to describe her experiences, with an extraordinary wealth of detail about her surroundings, and narrated remarkably emotional events. At first, I thought that her memories were merely fantasies, but Catherine began to improve after that session, and all of her symptoms eventually vanished as she recalled more past lives while under hypnosis. Within a few months, she was completely cured—without the use of any medication.

This series of events with Catherine (and subsequent patients) prompted a deep-rooted change in me. Although still somewhat skeptical, I searched through medical libraries and bookstores, seeking works that told of similar phenomena. I found some fairly good research, such as that by Dr. Ian Stevenson, who was chairman of the Department of Psychiatry at the University of Virginia. Dr. Stevenson wrote about some incidents involving children who were able to recall details of their earlier lives—these reports were later validated by thorough investigation. I'm certain that there are many additional medical professionals who are wary of telling the public about what they have observed in their practices, for they're frightened of losing their credibility. I know that I went through such a process: I waited five years before I wrote about my experiences with Catherine. I was fearful of damaging the reputation I had so carefully cultivated over many years of training and professional practice.

Now, there is no doubt in my mind that past-life regression therapy offers a rapid and effective way of treating physical and emotional symptoms, in addition to offering many other benefits. Thousands of patients— now with symptoms improved and fears and grief assuaged—attest to the power of this therapeutic technique.

Chapter Three

The

Benefits of Regression

*T*he path of our spiritual journey is an inward one, unique to each of us. Wise teachers can point the way, but only we can make the journey. We progress at our own speed, and there's no schedule or deadline for reaching enlightenment.

Regressing to significant childhood events, to infancy, or even to past lives may provide considerable relief and benefit in the present time. Sometimes, just through the act of remembering, symptoms can be removed. Memories can lead to understanding, and understanding frequently leads to healing.

You don't have to suffer from anything to receive benefits from the regression exercises contained within this book. You can recapture the happiness, joy, and spontaneity of childhood. You can even revisit loved ones—when you were all younger. You can remember past lifetimes, becoming aware through this process that your soul, your true essence, is immortal and eternal. You have lived before, and here you are again. You never really die, nor do your loved ones. You're always being reunited, either on the Other Side (in heaven) or back here in this physical dimension.

Whether you suffer from symptoms and fears, or whether you're just curious, there are many blessings awaiting you when you practice the regression exercises on the accompanying CD.

To some extent, frustration can block the healing and transformative process. Try not to expect specific results when using the CD. Just gently receive what comes to you. There is no time frame or race. Some people experience vivid memories or spiritual events the very first time; for others, it may take days, weeks, or even months. Many benefits will accrue even without memories. Just relax as much as possible, and open your mind to whatever enters your awareness. If you can practice with patience, you'll find much more joy, inner peace, and understanding in your life.

Chapter Four

Curing Fears and Phobias

*M*any people have already been practicing regression exercises by using my CDs and audiotapes, and they've related important memories that they've discovered in the process. Valuable recall—particularly memories related to phobias, pain, or other symptoms that we carry with us as a legacy from past lives—can lead to healing.

Relief from chronic musculoskeletal pain can occur quite rapidly when its past-life roots are uncovered.

For instance, a woman whom I had never met wrote to me saying that regression exercises had brought back a memory of having been hung in a previous life. After she made this discovery, the chronic pain in her neck—for which she had sought various forms of treatment to no avail—vanished. One interesting facet of her experience is that she discovered that she had been hung *unjustly* in this past life. Today, this woman is an advocate for the oppressed and the mistreated, a defender of human rights. When she remembered her past-life experience, she also understood her deeply ingrained inner drive to fight for the victimized.

I have regressed people suffering from asthma who were cured by recalling a death by fire or smoke inhalation in a past life. I also helped a young man who lost his fear of flying when he discovered that in a past life, he was the pilot of an aircraft shot down by the enemy in World War II.

Not everyone needs regression therapy—and even if no past-life memories are elicited, most people can profit greatly from simply practicing these exercises. In fact, approximately one-third of the people who do the exercises don't immediately have recollections of past lives. Nevertheless, the meditations offer other types of healing and benefits. For example, through the exercises, one can discover the power of mindful breathing, and one's muscles will learn the feeling of deep relaxation and the release of tension. Many people have written me to say that regularly practicing these exercises has helped them to deal far better with the stress and turbulence of their daily lives. They have subconsciously learned how to relax and release tension. During the course of the day, when facing moments that are particularly tense and stressful, these people just automatically breathe more deeply and consciously relax, which helps them to calm down and focus.

Physicians know that stress and anxiety can depress the immune system—therefore, achieving inner peace through these exercises can be very beneficial for one's health. In addition, inner peace allows love to flow freely, which doctors also know can prevent illness. The immunological system of people in love is functioning at its optimal level.

Even when there are no memories evoked, people suffering from anxiety and panic attacks can develop conscious control over their bodies through frequent practice of these exercises. They can learn to slow down their breathing and avoid hyperventilating. By controlling their respiratory rate, muscle tension, and even blood pressure, they're often able to halt these attacks.

I once treated a woman who suffered panic attacks when crossing bridges. Although she was unable to discover the origin of this problem, she developed such control over her breathing and the muscles of her body that she was able to prevent the attack from sweeping over her. She also became so mindful of the earliest physical sensations of an impending attack that she could virtually end the episode before it even began.

I have had many patients who have suffered heart attacks or are at high coronary risk, who come to me not specifically for regression, but rather to learn relaxation techniques. They want to control hypertension and stress-related events, particularly when side effects preclude taking medication. In many cases, people are unaware when their breathing accelerates or becomes irregular, which worsens their symptoms of stress. By practicing regression exercises, these individuals become much more aware of their breathing and also remain alert to other critical body signals—such as cardiac rhythm—which they gradually are able to control. I have also had many examples of those who found the motivation and willpower to lose weight, give up alcohol and drugs, and quit smoking. Others have managed to overcome insomnia. The bottom line is that regular practice of these exercises can greatly benefit both your body *and* your mind.

Chapter Five

Transforming

Relationships

As you perform the regression exercises, memories of past lives may occur, even if you're not particularly seeking them out. For example, a lawyer once consulted me because he was trying to resolve problems caused by hypertension. During our interview, he told me about the conflicts he was experiencing with his only son—which, the man confessed, were characterized by jealousy and competi-

tiveness on both sides. Through relaxation and regression exercises, his blood pressure improved, but
there was an unexpected bonus. While using the regression CD at home, a past-life memory emerged
that revealed the reasons behind his turbulent relationship with his son: In that life, both men had been
intense rivals, competing for the love of the same
woman. The understanding ushered in by the discovery of this ancient battle resulted in a complete change
in the man's behavior toward his son. Even though the
son had never undergone regression therapy himself,
he nevertheless reacted positively to the changes in his
father. The competition between them faded away,
for both men realized that it belonged in the past.
Consequently, love was able to flow between them
once again.

The deep relaxation achieved through the exercises is also able to release subconscious memories of childhood and promote emotional healing, for happy memories tend to remind us of loving moments and help to repair our self-esteem. In my book *Messages from the Masters,* I describe a hypnotic regression I performed on a television journalist, who recalled with much emotion the long, happy walks she used to take with her father along the streets of her hometown. This was a time for just the two of them to share, and the joy of this memory stayed with her even after the session ended. I was also able to help a woman who doubted the love of both of her parents and was afflicted by a problematic relationship with her mother. During a regression exercise, she relived the moment of her birth, and deeply felt the love and happiness with which her mother welcomed her into the world. This intense recollection and the emotion that it prompted triggered a drive in her to rebuild a closer and more loving relationship with her parents.

She could change the present (and also the future) by shifting her attitude and becoming more patient, loving, and forgiving toward her parents. In response to her new attitude, her parents were also able to express *their* love for her more directly.

There are countless cases where memories such as these help to reconcile parents and children, brothers and sisters, and husbands and wives. But even without specific recollections, the greater serenity, tolerance, and understanding achieved by practicing these exercises will benefit any relationship.

Chapter Six

A Shift in Values

One of the many benefits to be gained through meditation and regression is a shift in values, or a change in perspective that allows us to discern more clearly those things that are really important to us and those that aren't.

Such a shift in values can occur when we discover that we're immortal, that is, we don't die when our bodies do. When we experience past-life regression, we come to realize that we've lived before and we'll return to live again, united once more with our loved ones. The nature of suffering and mourning undergoes a transformation when we become aware that, although we may have lost *physical* contact with our family and friends, we will meet again on the Other Side or in another life.

The awareness that we are indeed spiritual beings prompts deep-rooted changes, leading us to greatly value such qualities as love, positive relationships, and compassion. We perceive our connection with all other beings more clearly. These new values subsequently become the foundation for happiness. Our priorities shift—events and people that previously upset or exasperated us can now be seen in a different light and from a different perspective. We become more patient and understanding. Our sense of inner peace and calm expands. The obstacles in our lives are now viewed more as opportunities to learn, stepping-stones along our evolutionary journey. After all, we're eternal, spiritual beings finding our way home—always loved and never alone. At this level, nothing can harm us.

As I mentioned previously, after years of being a skeptic, I now believe in past lives. My belief is due to 21 years of experience with thousands of patients. I have witnessed many extraordinary and incredible phenomena, but I don't feel that a belief in reincarnation is required for the benefits of regression therapy to accrue. Regardless of whether the material evoked is processed as metaphor or symbol, important information is brought to consciousness; the knowledge and insights gained can lead to significant physical, emotional, and spiritual transformations. Phobias and fears can vanish, values can change with this awakening to the spiritual dimension, love tends to flow more freely, and inner peace, which is connected to a sense of great joy and happiness, appears. The important point is not to be afraid, but to cast off prejudices and remain open-minded.

Chapter Seven

Appreciating

the Present

Another objective of the exercises contained within this book is to feel more peace, happiness, and joy in your current life—to enjoy your life *now*.

Believing that retrieving memories from the past can endow us with a keener awareness of the present may seem paradoxical, but it's the truth. We'll find that we become more adept at concentrating on and appreciating the current moment. On the one hand, the regression meditation is a focused-attention exercise, and its regular practice develops within us the capacity to concentrate on what's being felt and perceived now; but on the other hand, the memories that regression brings to the surface break through the walls that blind us to the present moment. As a result, we're no longer compelled to obsessively ruminate about the past or worry about the future. We're free to exist in the present, for only in the present can we experience joy.

Take, for example, the woman from Chapter 5 who had conflicts with her mother. When she ceased to be blinded by resentments from the past, she was able to perceive love in the present. We *all* tend to linger in the past and blame ourselves and others for faults committed, but, in addition to preventing us from enjoying more fully whatever the existing moment offers us, this clinging to the past is absolutely useless for solving any problems. With the memories that come to us during regressions, we'll discover one benefit of the past—that we can learn from it and accrue wisdom through experience so we may live better right now.

The same phenomenon occurs regarding the future. Just as ruminating over the past is useless, we discover that there is little point in worrying about the future, since that won't change whatever is going to happen. Planning for the future is necessary, but brooding about it is a waste of time. So freeing ourselves from the weight of the past and concern over the future enables us to concentrate on the present moment, the here-and-now.

Chapter Eight

Therapy and

Regression Exercises

*n*aturally, differences exist between using the regression CD included here and working with a psychotherapist who actually practices past-life regression therapy. But keep in mind that not everyone needs professional help.

If you're suffering from significant or severe psychological symptoms, using a therapist may be the wise choice, for the therapist can ask questions during the process and skillfully guide you through the regression process. The memories, feelings, and insights elicited during the session can then be interpreted and integrated by the therapist; therapeutic treatment and improvement will most likely follow. During our professional trainings, my wife, Carole, and I teach therapists how to apply the techniques of regression therapy in their clinical practices. We've found that well-trained therapists with carefully acquired clinical skills are best able to successfully incorporate past-life regression therapy into their practices. And the patients we refer to them tend to feel secure and receive excellent care.

However, if your symptoms are mild (or if you're merely curious), the regression CD is perfectly safe and can be very effective. Thousands of people have experienced distant childhood memories—or even their first past-life recall—while using the CD. There's no danger in listening to it, although *you should not listen to the CD while driving a car.* Occasionally, you may go too deep and fall asleep while listening; this effect can be minimized by not listening at night or when tired, or by listening while sitting rather than lying down.

With practice, the experiences will become more detailed and vivid. It's important to remain patient— just keep practicing without any timetable or expectations, and sooner or later, you will see results.

The following is an example of someone who noticed marked improvement after listening to the CD.

I once heard from a woman who suffered from claustrophobia. During regression, she remembered that in a lifetime in ancient Egypt, she was a servant in the household of a nobleman . . . and she was buried alive. The nobleman she served had died, and it was the custom of that culture to bury slaves, servants, and treasures with the deceased so that they would be available to him when he reached "the Other

Side." Ancient Egyptians believed that you really *could* take it with you! In that life, the woman died from suffocation in the burial chamber, and that trauma resulted in her present-day fear.

Although this woman experienced much emotion while remembering this scene and the panic of being suffocated, she felt that she was in control of the depth of her feelings, so she chose to stay with the sensation and experience it again. Remembering that lifetime, with its accompanying feelings, gave her a greater understanding that her fear had come from the past; it most certainly was not related to the present or the future. And so, her phobia disappeared.

Please remember that if you're ever uncomfortable with any memory or experience while listening to the CD, you can just float above the scene and observe it from a distance, as if you're watching a movie.

Or, you can open your eyes and end the process at any time. Detach from the emotions—*you are always in control*.

If you're comfortable during the regression process, pay attention to any details you notice, whether they're visual or otherwise. You'll be amazed at what you can experience and learn. Symptoms and fears may dramatically improve, and you may even catch a glimpse of your true spiritual nature.

Chapter Nine

Relaxation

and Hypnosis

*T*he state of pleasant relaxation induced by listening to the CD is similar to the light hypnotic trance brought about by progressive relaxation techniques. Hypnosis is actually a type of focused concentration while someone is relaxed—which is something we all experience, every single day. For example, when you're so absorbed in a book or movie that you don't get distracted by the everyday noises around you—be it traffic or people talking or coughing—you're in a light hypnotic trance.

But thanks to what we've seen on TV or in the movies, there are many myths about hypnosis. In reality, *all* hypnosis is self-hypnosis. The hypnotist is merely a facilitator who helps the person reach a level of moderate to deep relaxation. "Stage hypnotists," however, have taken relaxed attention or concentration (which is a natural ability) and transformed it into entertainment. And so, because of the many erroneous associations to the word *hypnosis,* the term *relaxed focused concentration* may instead be preferable, but they both mean the same thing. In this state, the memory is enhanced and people are able to recall events and incidents that may have been long forgotten. Sometimes, due to their expanded understanding of life, people have spiritual or intuitive experiences that they greatly benefit from.

Since this state of relaxed concentration is entirely normal, there is no danger. You can return to full waking consciousness whenever you choose. It's very important to keep the following things in mind: (1) You can never get "stuck" in the hypnotic state, because it's only a form of focused concentration—you can open your eyes and end the process at any time; (2) *you are always in control;* (3) you can never do anything against your will or values; (4) you won't do or say something in an unaware state, for hypnosis isn't sleep—the person is always aware of their thoughts and their subconscious mind remains active and alert; and (5) the process is like a daydream—not anesthesia.

Just try to keep an open mind. There's nothing to fear or to lose—and what you gain may greatly improve the quality of your life.

PART II

Addressing

Your Concerns

Chapter Ten

Questions

People Often Ask

*T*his part of the book contains answers to some of the most frequently asked questions I hear concerning hypnosis, regression, and reincarnation. Because concerns, doubts, and fears may block someone from experiencing the full efficacy and enjoyment of the regression CD, this chapter should help to remove those possible barriers and may also explain some of the phenomena that occur.

Q. Do the regression exercises always evoke memories of past lives? Is this the only way to have such memories?

A. It's certainly possible to have actual past-life recall through these regression exercises, although many other types of relaxation or meditation techniques can lead to the same thing as well. People may also experience past-life recall during dreams or déjà vu, spontaneously (this is often seen with children), or in many other ways. For example, my first recollection of a past life actually didn't take place during regression therapy or hypnosis, but as a result of the state of relaxation caused by shiatsu massage (or acupressure). Suddenly, I vividly observed myself as a priest in ancient Babylon. Now, for those of you who feel discouraged because you can't seem to bring back memories of past lives when you first use the CD, I'd like to point out that it took me *three months* of daily meditation before I had this first regression. So, the more you practice, the better prepared you'll be to open up to these experiences.

Keep in mind that the CD might not lead to a memory of a past life at all; or you may retrieve a memory from your childhood, where the causes of your current problem may lie. The wisdom of the subconscious will take us wherever we need to go for the cure to take place.

Q. Do the regression exercises offer any type of risk if I do them alone?

A. Thousands of my patients, readers, and workshop participants have used these exercises without any problems, because the subconscious offers powerful protection against distressing feelings or experiences. Therefore, nothing too traumatic will enter your awareness. If anything uncomfortable arises in the regression exercises, I instruct you to detach from the scene and float above it, where you can view it without emotion.

You can also open your eyes and end the experience. The choice is always there. The only risk lies in doing the exercises while driving a car or handling equipment that needs your full attention.

❧❧ ❧❧

Q. *Do you need to achieve a deep level of focused relaxation to experience past-life regression?*

A. No—even people with a moderate response can experience the benefits.

❧❧ ❧❧

Q. *What are the memories like that come during regression?*

A. I find that actual past-life memories are usually accessed and described in one of two ways. The first is the **classical** pattern, where the person enters one lifetime only and is able to perceive an extremely complete, detailed depiction of that life and its events. Almost as if it were a story, much of the *entire* lifetime passes by; that is, it often begins with birth or childhood and doesn't end until death. It's possible that the person will painlessly and serenely experience the death scene and a life review, where the lessons of the lifetime are illuminated and explored with the benefit of the person's higher wisdom and possibly by a religious figure or spiritual guide.

The second pattern of past-life recall is what I call the **key-moment flow.** Here, the subconscious knits together the most important or related moments from a cluster of lifetimes, those key points that best elucidate the person's hidden trauma and can most quickly and powerfully heal them.

Q. *I can recall just short moments of previous lives—will that help me?*

A. Remembering these "short moments" is often enough to give you insight into your present life and to open your mind to the possibility of soul survival, reincarnation, and the like.

Q. *How can I know if the memories I have are real, or if they're fantasies or the result of my imagination?*

A. It isn't critical to determine whether what comes to mind is a symbol, a metaphor, a true memory, your imagination, or a mixture of them all. My advice is to relax and let what happens happen, in a nonjudgmental way. If you allow the rational side of your brain to take over, you may block memories and waste an opportunity. Just *experience* and let your superconscious wisdom come—afterwards, you can analyze what you've gone through. With practice, things become clearer, and you can differentiate what is memory and what is metaphor, symbol, or imagination.

There are many people who try to validate their memories with proof: Some of them have found their own graves; others find official records that confirm evidential details of their recall, offering proof of past lives. One of the most extraordinary cases of this involves a woman named Jenny Cockell. As a child, she had memories of living in Ireland and dying when her children were still small. As an adult, she decided to look for them, and she managed to find five of the eight children that she had borne during that life.

Validation may also take place through the intensity of the feelings associated with the memory and by the alleviation of symptoms. Xenoglossy, which is the ability to fluently speak a language one has never learned or even encountered, is another type of proof.

Q. What's the reason for using images of light, a staircase, and a garden during the process?

A. The image of the light (and its symbolism) is found in all cultures and societies on our planet. In near-death experiences, a magnificent light often appears as the consciousness detaches from the physical body. The light transmits the feeling of peace and is associated with understanding. And just like color, light is a form of energy. I like to use light and colors to deepen the induction to regression, and as a metaphor for opening up the mind and enhancing perception.

As for the staircase, slowly descending it symbolically leads to deeper awareness and concentration. The garden is a metaphor for a safe harbor, or the place where one feels protected and secure from any danger. This is why I sometimes recommend that when people experience anxiety and tension, they should breathe in deeply, imagine themselves immersed in light, and visualize the garden of safety and serenity.

Q. What happens if I'm unable to visualize the symbols that appear in the exercise?

A. Remember that the other senses also count—the experience doesn't have to be visual. For instance, during the process, people have described that they "knew" or "felt" the symbols.

Q. How frequently should the exercises be done?

A. The more you do them, the more experiences you may have, and the deeper you'll be able to go. This means that it would be ideal to meditate with the exercises every day, particularly because it's healthy for the body and mind to have a half hour of relaxation and concentration amidst all the tumult and stress of daily life. But if you take long breaks between the exercises, don't give up—simply go back to doing them, without judgment or guilt.

Q. Does everyone reincarnate?

A. Reincarnation occurs because we have lessons to learn about such things as love, compassion, charity, nonviolence, inner peace, and patience—it would be hard to master them all in only one life. If your education isn't finished, you'll find yourself being born into another lifetime. There may be some choices involved, however, but apparently these choices are limited. For example, when you learn all about love, you don't have to come back. Yet highly evolved souls often voluntarily choose to reincarnate to help teach others.

Q. Where do the souls come from if there are more people on Earth now than ever before?

A. I've posed this question to many patients, and the answer is always the same: This isn't the only place where there are souls. There are many dimensions and different levels of consciousness where souls exist. Why should we feel that we're the only place for souls? After all, there's no limit to energy. Earth is merely one of many schools in the universe. In addition, a few patients have told me that souls can "split" and have simultaneous experiences.

Q. In Many Lives, Many Masters, *Catherine remembered a lifetime in 1863 B.C. How could she know that it was B.C. when that wasn't even a concept yet?*

A. In *Through Time into Healing,* I explain the process of hypnotism in more detail:

> Your conscious mind is always aware of what you are experiencing while you are hypnotized. Despite the deep subconscious contact, your mind can comment, criticize, and censor. . . . Some people in hypnosis watch the past as if they are observing a movie. . . . In hypnosis, your mind is always aware and observing. This is why people who may be deeply hypnotized and actively involved in a childhood or past-life sequence of memories are able to answer the therapist's questions, speak their current life language, know the geographical places they are seeing, and even know the year, which usually flashes before their inner eyes or just appears in their minds. The hypnotized mind, *always retaining an awareness and knowledge of the present,* puts the childhood or past-life memories into context. If the year 1900 flashes, and you find yourself building a pyramid in ancient Egypt, you *know* that the year is B.C., even if you don't see those actual letters.

Q. Does past-life regression therapy conflict with other psychotherapeutic techniques?

A. Regression therapy is very similar to traditional psychotherapy and psychoanalysis. When traumatic events are brought to the surface, interpreted, and integrated, clinical improvement usually results. The main difference is that regression therapy enlarges the arena, so memories can be retrieved not just from this life but from previous lives as well.

Q. Do animals have souls? Do they reincarnate?

A. I think that animals do have souls. At least this comes up in my work from time to time. I'm not sure that their souls are as individuated as ours—there may be more emphasis on a group soul. I'm also unsure about animal reincarnation, but I'm open to the

67

possibility. Becoming aware of a pet or beloved animal after crossing to the Other Side is a frequent occurrence. However, I'm not convinced that people reincarnate as animals or plants. Perhaps they do, but the memory from those states isn't retained.

Q. Is it possible to go into future lives?

A. It *is* possible to go into the future, and some people spontaneously do, but I don't pursue that area for several reasons. For instance, there seem to be *possible* futures and *probable* futures. Also, there may be distortions related to going into the future, and you might make decisions that you don't need to make. You absolutely need to have reached a certain level of maturity in order to "go into the future."

I think that destiny and choice both exist and keep interacting with each other, because as soon as you make a choice, it changes the future. So maybe the possibilities and probabilities change to an extent as you do that. It's true that we learn because of free choice, but we also can't discount the role destiny plays in our lives.

Q. Is a past-life reading from a psychic as valuable as experiencing one's own regression?

A. Although information from a psychic is interesting and sometimes informative, it usually doesn't remove symptoms. For in order to get resolution, you should experience the memory, with its accompanying emotion, yourself. Your own experience of the memory through regression will be much richer, deeper, and more personal. It will contain a feeling of "knowing" that a simple reading would never be able to convey.

Chapter Eleven

In the

Mirrors of Time

*"You are much, much more than your body or
your mind. You are a beautiful being,
immortal, eternal, full of love and light."*
— Brian Weiss

*T*he quest for happiness is a common denomi-
nator among all human beings. Driven by this
desire, we create new technologies and fine-
tune existing techniques in order to reach levels of extraordinary sophistication in the consumption of

consumer goods. Yet, despite the incredible sophistication of our society, I feel that there is widespread dissatisfaction on the individual level. Having more, earning more, needing more; and being better, more famous, more brilliant, and more successful than everybody else are just superficial attempts to find happiness—but these social differences are creating wider and wider chasms among people. In addition, our society is seriously threatening the planet and rapidly poisoning the environment.

At the same time, a spiritual revolution is occurring. It seems to me that the people who read my books, attend my lectures, or write to me are trying to do far more than solve mere physical or emotional problems. They're seeking a pathway to endow their lives with more meaning, fulfillment, and joy, and they're transcending the mundane. For me, the essence of happiness is inner peace. And this peace can be achieved only when we recognize our fundamental nature, which is unconditional love: love that's freely expressed and asks for nothing in return.

This is what we came to learn in this school of life, and we need many lives to accumulate this wisdom. As this is not an easy school, and the process takes much time, advances are often imperceptible, while lapses may well discourage us.

It's worthwhile to invest in this path of love, however, because it's one of peace and happiness. Don't worry about the pace of progress or judge yourself when you make mistakes. This is *your* unique path, and there's so much to learn along the way. In this school, we have physical bodies and we learn through emotions and relationships. As we progress along the path of spirituality, we'll become more tolerant, understanding, and open to love.

I want to offer you my support and encouragement and be a companion for you on this journey. Be persistent, patient, and open—the journey truly is as important as the destination.

Appendix

Regression CD: Transcript

*[**Editor's Note:** We have included the text of the CD in case you would like to follow along or would like to refer back to it at a future date.]*

*B*egin by focusing on your breath . . . going deeply within. . . . With each breath, let yourself go deeper and deeper . . . into a beautiful, relaxed, serene state, deeper and deeper within. . . . Focus on your breathing. . . . This is called "Yoga breathing," an ancient technique. . . . Deeper and deeper with each breath. . . .

As you do this, relax all of your muscles, and feel yourself going even deeper. . . . Relax your facial muscles and jaw . . . a lot of tension is stored in this area. . . . Relax all the muscles of your neck . . . this area stores a great deal of anxiety and tension. People with headaches from neck pain carry a great deal of tension in their necks. Relax these muscles completely. . . .

And now, relax the muscles of your shoulders. Let them feel light, loose . . . completely relaxed. People who walk around with the weight of the world on their shoulders have tightness and tension in these muscles. . . .

Relax the muscles of your arms and of your back . . . both the upper back and lower back . . . completely relaxing. . . . Relax the muscles of your stomach so that your breathing stays beautifully relaxed . . . deep . . . even. . . .

And lastly, relax the muscles of your legs. . . . Completely relaxing your whole body now . . . unwinding . . . going deeper . . . relaxing completely. . . .

Feel yourself going even deeper. . . .

Next, visualize a beautiful light coming in through the top of your head and beginning to gently spread down your body from above to below . . . entering your brain, your nervous system, glowing beautifully in the light. You choose the color or colors. . . . This is a powerful, healing, relaxing light . . . connected with the light above and around you. . . .

And it flows down beneath the deep bones and muscles of your face . . . into your jaw, the back of your head, as you go deeper and deeper . . . and it flows into your neck, relaxing all of these muscles and nerves . . . and in your throat, it smooths the lining of your throat. And you go even deeper. . . .

And it flows into your shoulders and down your arms, healing and relaxing every muscle, every nerve, every fiber, and every cell of your body. Reaching to your hands and your fingers, as you go deeper and deeper. . . .

And it flows from your shoulders, down your back, healing and relaxing these large muscles and nerves and the spinal cord in this region. . . .

And it flows into your chest, filling your lungs, glowing beautifully in the light, healing . . . and filling your heart, healing your heart, releasing the beautiful energy, which is stored in your heart. . . . And your heart, gently pumping the light throughout every blood vessel of your body so that it reaches everywhere, and you feel so peaceful, so deeply relaxed, so serene, so calm. . . .

Focus on my voice, letting other noises or distractions only deepen your level even more as they fade away. . . .

And the light flowing into your stomach and abdomen, filling up all of the abdominal organs and healing them. . . . And relaxing the nerves, the muscles of your stomach and abdomen. . . .

And the light flowing past your hips . . . and down both legs. This beautiful, healing, deepening, relaxing light . . . filling every cell, every fiber of your body with beautiful calm. Getting rid of all illness and restoring every tissue, every cell, every organ to the normal, healthy state. . . .

And the light reaches to your feet and your toes, filling your body. And you feel so peaceful, so relaxed, so deeply, deeply calm. Let yourself go even deeper. . . .

And next, visualize, imagine the light completely surrounding the outside of your body as well, as if you were in a bubble or a halo of light. And this protects you. No harm can come through the light, only goodness, only positive, loving energy. . . .

And the light heals your skin and outer muscles and deepens your level even more. . . .

In a few moments, I am going to count backwards from ten to one. With each number back, let yourself go even deeper. So deep that by the time I reach one, you are in a state of deep peace, tranquility, and relaxation. So deep that your mind is no longer limited by the usual barriers of space or of time. So deep that you can remember everything—every experience that you've ever had, no matter when. . . . So deep that you can experience all levels of your multidimensional self. . . .

Ten . . . nine . . . eight . . . going deeper and deeper with each number back . . . seven . . . six . . . five . . . deeper and deeper and deeper . . . four . . . three . . . so deep, so peaceful, so relaxed and calm . . . two . . . nearly there . . . one . . . good.

In this beautiful state of peace and relaxation, imagine yourself, visualize yourself, walking down a beautiful staircase . . . down, down, deeper and deeper . . . down . . . down . . . each step down increasing even more the depth of your level. . . .

And as you reach the bottom of the stairs, in front of you is a beautiful, magnificent garden. A garden of peace and safety, of serenity and tranquility. . . . Go into this garden. . . . It is a garden filled with beautiful flowers, plants, trees, grass, fountains, benches, and places to rest. . . . Find a place to rest, and let your body completely unwind, continuing to heal, filled with the beautiful light. Your body will refresh, relax, recuperate, rejuvenate. Later on, after you are awake, you will feel wonderful, filled with the beautiful energy. Even though wide awake and alert and in full control of your body and your mind, you'll feel wonderful, so relaxed and so peaceful. The deepest, deepest levels of your mind can open up. You can remember everything. . . .

To show you this, let us go back in time. . . . Let us go back to your childhood. . . . As you stay in the deeply relaxed, calm, and peaceful state . . . let your deepest mind pick out a childhood memory. If you wish, you can keep it a pleasant memory . . . but you are free to choose. If at any time you become uncomfortable, just imagine yourself back in the garden, resting. . . . You are always in control. . . . If you wish, you can just float above the scene, watching it, as if from a distance. . . . Or, you can be in it, feeling it, seeing it vividly with colors and details, with emotions and feelings. This is up to you. Go back to your childhood, pick out a memory.

It may be something you have not thought about or remembered for a long, long time. . . .

Spend a few moments here . . . remembering vividly, seeing, feeling, using all of your senses. . . .

Now, let us go back even earlier, to a younger age, as an infant or a toddler or a small child, and pick out another memory, and again remember it vividly, using all of your senses—sight, sound, taste, touch, smell. Be there! Experience it. Remember—you can always float above it or, if uncomfortable, just come back into the garden. . . .

Do not worry what is imagination, fantasy, or actual memory. This is all coming from your mind. It is all important. It is all from you, and it may be a mixture of all of these. This is for the experience. . . . Let yourself experience. Let yourself remember. . . . Stay in a deep state and reexperience these memories. . . .

There is no limit to your memory. You can go back as far as you wish. . . . In this lifetime, you can go back to infancy, to birth, perhaps even in utero. . . . There is no limit, and you can remember everything. . . .

If you wish to go further . . . we can do that now. . . .

Imagine now that you are back in the garden . . . and in front of you is a large and beautiful mirror . . . filled with light. And as you look into this mirror, you see the reflections of many, many mirrors. And in each of these mirrors, you are in a different time, a different place . . . perhaps a different space or dimension . . . perhaps another lifetime. If you wish, you will be able to go back and remember this now. . . .

As I count backwards from five to one, feel yourself being drawn, pulled to one of these mirrors, one of these reflections. As you look back, you can see yourself in many, many different places, times, in different dress. You may look very different. You will be drawn, pulled to one of these mirrors, to one of these times. Perhaps one that helps you to explain or understand a problem, a symptom, a talent, a relationship, a habit, special knowledge, whatever it is. Feel yourself pulled, drawn to one of these or several of these. And as I count backwards from five to one, go into this mirror. Again, if you feel at all uncomfortable, just float above and watch it, as if watching a movie. But if you wish, you can be within, experiencing vividly. . . .

As I count backwards, go into the mirrors. Enter the reflection which pulls you . . . to help you understand, and by understanding, to remove any blocks, any obstacles to your inner peace and joy, to your inner happiness. . . .

Five . . . four . . . three . . . going into the mirror . . . being drawn . . . two . . . nearly through . . . one . . . be there!

If you have a body, look down at your feet and see what you are wearing on your feet, whether shoes or sandals or furs or skin or perhaps nothing at all. And look up your body. Look at your skin, your clothes, your hands, the size, the color. And look around at the topography, the geography. Are there buildings, are there people? Find yourself . . . let a date come into your head, into your mind. Where are you?

You can move forward or backward in time. . . . Go to significant events. Spend as much time as you need . . . and find the answers. . . .

If you wish, you can move forward in time and find out what happens, what happens to you. Are there any traumas? Is there a death scene? If you wish not to view this, not to experience this, then do not. Just float above. If you feel drawn to more than one time, you can do this, too. You can travel. You can see more then one lifetime. But if you choose to stay and in more detail examine one, that is fine. . . . Take as much time as you need. . . .

Pay attention to details. To clothes, to dress, to appearances. . . . You will be able to remember everything. . . .

Soon, it is time to come back . . . and imagine that you are now finishing up and leaving this time or these times . . . and returning to the garden where your body has been resting and refreshing and healing. . . .

And now, it is time to awaken . . . and I will awaken you by counting up from one to ten. When I say ten, you can open your eyes. You'll be awake and alert, in full control of your body and your mind. Feeling wonderful, refreshed, relaxed, filled with the beautiful energy. Feeling great.

One . . . two . . . three . . . more and more awake
and alert, feeling wonderful . . . four . . . five . . . six
. . . more and more awake, feeling great . . . seven . . .
eight . . . nearly awake now . . . nine . . . ten.

About the Author

Brian L. Weiss, M.D., maintains a private practice in Miami, Florida, where his offices include well-trained and highly experienced psychologists and social workers who also use regression therapy and the techniques of spiritual psychotherapy in their work. In addition, Dr. Weiss conducts national and international seminars and experiential workshops as well as training programs for professionals.

Other meditation and regression audiotapes and CDs are available. For more information, please contact:

The Weiss Institute
6701 Sunset Drive, Suite 201
Miami, FL 33143
Phone: (305) 661-6610
Fax: (305) 661-5311
e-mail: in2healing@aol.com
www.brianweiss.com

(The exercise on the enclosed CD was previously available through The Weiss Institute as *Regression Through the Mirrors of Time*.)

Other Hay House Titles of Related Interest

BOOKS

Chakra Clearing, by Doreen Virtue, Ph.D.

Infinite Self, by Stuart Wilde

The Lightworker's Way: Awakening Your Spiritual Power to Know and Heal, by Doreen Virtue, Ph.D.

Meditations, by Sylvia Browne

The Reconnection: Heal Others, Heal Yourself, by Dr. Eric Pearl

Sixth Sense, by Stuart Wilde

Visionseeker: Shared Wisdom from the Place of Refuge, by Hank Wesselman, Ph.D.

You Can Heal Your Life Companion Book, by Louise L. Hay

AUDIO PROGRAMS

Intuitive Healing: Five Steps to Developing Intuition,
by Judith Orloff, M.D.

Journeys into Past Lives, by Denise Linn

Karma Releasing, by Doreen Virtue, Ph.D.

Past-Life Regression with the Angels,
by Doreen Virtue, Ph.D.

Sylvia Browne's Tools for Life, by Sylvia Browne

Your Journey to Enlightenment,
by Dr. Wayne W. Dyer

CARD DECKS

The Four Agreements Cards,
by DON Miguel Ruiz

Healing with the Angels Oracle Cards,
by Doreen Virtue, Ph.D.

Inner Peace Cards, by Dr. Wayne W. Dyer

Zen Cards, by Daniel Levin

All of these titles are available at your local bookstore,
or may be ordered through Hay House, Inc.:

(800) 654-5126 or (760) 431-7695
(800) 650-5115 (fax) or (760) 431-6948 (fax)
www.hayhouse.com

We hope you enjoyed this Hay House book.
If you would like to receive a free catalog featuring additional
Hay House books and products, or if you would like information
about the Hay Foundation, please contact:

Hay House, Inc.
P.O. Box 5100
Carlsbad, CA 92018-5100

(760) 431-7695 or **(800) 654-5126**
(760) 431-6948 (fax) or **(800) 650-5115 (fax)**

Hay House Australia Pty Ltd
P.O. Box 515
Brighton-Le-Sands NSW 2216
phone: 1800 023 516
e-mail: info@hayhouse.com.au

Please visit the Hay House Website at: **www.hayhouse.com**